THE
HUSTLE

Unleashing Your Potential Beyond Military Service

First Published in 2023
Published by Forky Publishing

Paperback ISBN: 978-1-7395532-0-3
eBook ISBN: 978-1-7395532-1-0

Cover Design and Book Layout by:
SpiffingCovers.com

THE HUSTLE

Unleashing Your Potential Beyond Military Service

MATT J. JOHNSTON

For Sunday and Verity.

Contents

FOREWORD

"Every man thinks meanly of himself for not having
been a soldier, or not having been at sea."
– Samuel Johnson.

In this book, we embark on a transformative journey, exploring the power of the hustle and its profound impact on the lives of military service leavers. Drawing from my personal experiences of coming from a traditional working-class background to my situation today, I will share insights, strategies and valuable lessons to help you unleash your true potential and enable you to become part of the top 1% of earners in the country. The hustle is not merely about money; it is about embracing a mindset that propels you toward fulfilling your dreams and achieving the success you deserve.

Over the past few years, since leaving the military, I have dedicated myself to coaching and mentoring service leavers who are transitioning into civilian life. Leaving the military was a challenging time for me as well, as I left straight into a pandemic, uncertain of what the future held. With a family to support, I knew I had to create a method for success – it was sink or swim. As I persevered and navigated through the difficulties, I began to achieve my goals and establish a fulfilling career outside the military. My success didn't go unnoticed, and soon friends and colleagues started approaching me, asking how I managed to create my own path. I realised that the strategies and techniques I had developed were not only effective for myself but could also benefit others. It brings me great joy to see my friends and colleagues now flourishing in their own endeavours, having applied the methods I shared with them. And now I am thrilled to share this method with you, as I believe it can empower and guide you towards your own success in life after the military.

Leaving the military behind is not just a transition; it is a chance for reinvention. As service leavers, we possess a unique set of skills, values and experiences that can set us apart in the civilian world. We will explore the essence of the hustle and its significance in your post-military journey. By harnessing the power of the hustle, you can overcome challenges, embrace your worth, let go of old hierarchies, stay true to your values and apply the processes learned during your military career.

Through the chapters ahead, we will delve into the hustle's relentless nature, the importance of self-worth, cultivating ruthless efficiency, and ultimately finding your own 'milk and honey'.

CHAPTER 1
The Hustle Never Sleeps

"Success is no accident. It is hard work, perseverance,
learning, studying, sacrifice and most of all,
love of what you are doing." – Pelé

In the military, we learn the value of discipline and commitment. The hustle demands that same unwavering dedication. It recognises that success is not handed to us; it is earned through continuous effort, constant learning and a burning passion for our goals. The hustle never sleeps; it drives us to push beyond our limits, to embrace challenges and to persist even when the path ahead seems arduous. It is in the pursuit of our dreams that we uncover our true potential and find fulfilment.

Success is not a destination but a journey, one that requires continuous learning, adaptation and the willingness to evolve. It is through this constant pursuit of growth that we uncover hidden talents and capabilities we never knew we possessed.

The hustle is not limited to a particular time or place. It transcends boundaries and permeates all aspects of our lives. It is a mindset that drives us to give our all, whether we are working on our professional goals, personal aspirations or relationships. It teaches us that success is not limited to a specific domain but can be achieved in all areas of life through dedication and perseverance.

When I fully embraced the hustle, I became unstoppable. I developed a burning passion for my goals, and that passion became the fuel that propelled me forward. I no longer viewed challenges as setbacks but as opportunities for growth and achievement. With this mindset, I can teach you to persist even when the path seems arduous, knowing that the rewards are worth the effort.

As military service leavers, we bring with us a unique set of skills and experiences that can be leveraged. Our training has taught us resilience, adaptability and the ability to thrive in high-pressure situations. These qualities give us an edge in the civilian world, allowing us to tackle challenges with confidence and overcome obstacles with determination.

In the pursuit of our dreams, we uncover not only our true potential but also a deep sense of fulfilment. It's more than just material success; it is about finding purpose and meaning in our endeavours. It is about aligning our actions with our values and making a positive impact on the world around us.

This will challenge us to go beyond what is expected of us, to surpass our own limitations, and to redefine what is possible. It encourages us to take risks, step out of our comfort zones and embrace the unknown. Never settle for mediocrity.

The hustle is a mindset that empowers us to live life to the fullest. It is a constant reminder that success is not handed to us but earned through hard work, determination and a burning desire to make our dreams a reality.

The power of visualisation has been instrumental in helping me achieve numerous goals and overcome challenges. By vividly imagining myself succeeding and visualising the steps I needed to take, I was able to create a clear roadmap towards my objectives. Visualisation allowed me to stay focused, motivated and confident in the face of obstacles, as it provided a mental image of my desired outcome. This technique not only enhanced my performance but also helped me tap into my subconscious mind, aligning my thoughts and actions with my goals. By doing this, I transformed my aspirations into reality, harnessing the power of my imagination to shape my path towards success.

Make time for visualisation. For me, this takes place every morning whilst enjoying a coffee and staring out into the garden. No noise, no distractions – just thought.

CHAPTER 2
Know Your Worth

"Know your worth and then add tax." – Anonymous

As military service leavers, it is easy to underestimate our value in the civilian world. However, we possess a unique set of skills, discipline and resilience that few can match. Knowing your worth means recognising the immense potential within you and refusing to settle for less than what you deserve. You must confidently assert yourself, negotiate for what you're worth and seize opportunities that align with your true potential. By recognising and harnessing your worth, you can unlock doors to success you never thought possible.

We have been moulded by the military to thrive in demanding environments. Recognising our worth is crucial to thriving in civilian life.

In the civilian world, it can be easy to succumb to self-doubt, feeling as though we lack the qualifications or experience to compete with our civilian counterparts. However, the hustle teaches us that our military background equips us with a unique skill set that is highly valuable. Our ability to adapt quickly, make sound decisions under pressure and work effectively in teams are qualities that make us stand out in various industries.

We may have expertise in leadership, strategic thinking, problem-solving and teamwork, which are highly sought after in many professional arenas. Embracing our worth means understanding that we bring a distinct perspective and a valuable set of skills to the table.

By recognising and harnessing our worth, we open doors to success that we may have never thought possible. It starts with building self-awareness and reflecting on our accomplishments and capabilities. We must take inventory of the challenges we have overcome, the skills we have developed, and the impact we have made during our military service. Understanding the value we bring allows us to confidently pursue opportunities that align with our goals and aspirations.

It is essential to invest time and effort into personal development. This may involve upskilling, acquiring new certifications or pursuing higher education. By continuously expanding our knowledge and enhancing our skill set, we not only increase our worth but also position ourselves as valuable assets in the job market.

I also encourage you to seek mentorship and guidance from those who have successfully transitioned from military to civilian life. Mentors can provide valuable insights, support and advice as we navigate our new environment. They can help us identify our strengths and weaknesses, develop effective strategies and unlock our full potential.

Part of recognising our worth is also understanding the importance of networking. By building connections with professionals in our desired industries, attending events and engaging with online communities, we expand our opportunities for success. Networking allows us to showcase our unique qualities and capabilities while connecting with individuals who may offer guidance, referrals or even potential job opportunities. In short, stay in touch with your mates and ask for course notes!

Embracing our worth is about realising that we are deserving of success, both personally and professionally. It is about challenging the self-limiting beliefs that may hold us back and stepping into our power. We must embrace our strengths, assert ourselves and pursue the opportunities that align with our true potential. By recognising and harnessing our worth, we can confidently navigate the challenges of the civilian world and unlock a future filled with possibilities.

I spend a lot of time with service leavers discussing exactly how much they are worth. Objectively, and as a commodity, we are all highly prized assets. When you get asked the question 'what is your salary expectation?', make sure that you've given yourself the appropriate appraisal! You're no longer trapped on a 'time served, pyramid' pay spine. Be bold (and don't leave money on the table).

CHAPTER 3
Forget About Rank

"In the hustle, there are no ranks, only results." —
Anonymous

The military instils a strong sense of hierarchy, where rank defines our positions and responsibilities. However, in the civilian world, the hustle knows no rank. It is up to us to shed the limitations imposed by hierarchical structures and embrace a mindset that values merit, initiative and results. Letting go of rank allows us to explore new avenues, take risks and forge our own paths. By focusing on our capabilities and achievements, rather than our previous military roles, we can unleash our full potential and redefine our own success.

Letting go of rank is liberating. By releasing ourselves from the expectations and constraints associated with rank, we open ourselves up to endless possibilities. The hustle beckons us to take risks, venture into uncharted territory, and forge our own paths based on our unique capabilities and aspirations.

Embracing a mindset that values merit, initiative and results empowers us to create our own opportunities. We no longer wait for orders or rely solely on the recognition bestowed upon us by our superiors. Instead, we take ownership of our journey and proactively seek ways to make a significant impact.

Breaking free from the confines of rank also allows us to embrace a more holistic view of success. In the military, promotions and advancements are often tied to specific roles or positions. However, the hustle recognises that success is not limited to climbing a predetermined ladder. It is about finding contentment and achieving excellence in various aspects of life, including our personal relationships, health and overall well-being. By focusing on our capabilities and achievements beyond our military roles, we open ourselves up to a broader definition of success.

When we let go of rank, we create an environment that fosters innovation and collaboration. Ideas and contributions are valued based on their merit, rather than the position from which they originate. This promotes a culture of inclusivity, where diverse perspectives are encouraged and fresh ideas are welcomed. By embracing this mindset, we can tap into our collective potential, break down silos and create breakthrough solutions.

Evolving away from rank also allows us to approach challenges and setbacks with resilience and adaptability. In the military, our rank may serve as a safety net, providing a sense of security and stability. However, when we hustle, we must rely on our own abilities to navigate through uncertain terrain. This requires us to embrace change, learn from failures and continuously adapt our strategies. By embracing a rankless mindset, we become more agile and better equipped to thrive in dynamic and evolving environments.

Shedding the limitations imposed by hierarchical structures enables us to transcend the boundaries of traditional career paths. The hustle encourages us to explore unconventional avenues and create our own opportunities. It empowers us to pursue our passions and leverage our unique skill set in ways that align with our personal aspirations. By focusing on our capabilities and achievements rather than adhering to predefined career trajectories, we can uncover hidden talents and discover new paths to success.

Embracing a rankless mindset in the hustle is about reclaiming our agency and defining our own narrative. It is about recognising that success is not limited to the position or rank we held in the military, but rather the impact we make and the value we bring to the table. By embracing our individual potential, taking risks and forging our own paths, we unleash our full capabilities and redefine what success means to us in the civilian world.

The legends are true. Outside of the military, rank is meaningless. In this brave new world, junior soldiers have just as fair a shot at the best jobs – and the big bucks – as senior officers. I find this so refreshing. A world where people are judged by what they do, rather than how long they've been in the organisation. Clearly there's always room for a bit of banter and I love telling people that I 'used to work for a living', but the hustle doesn't care what rank you were, it only cares about what type of hustle you have.

CHAPTER 4
Maintain Your Values

"Your beliefs don't make you a better person;
your behaviour does." – Sukhraj S. Dhillon

Our military service instils core values such as courage, discipline, integrity and selflessness. As we transition into civilian life, it is crucial to maintain these values while navigating the hustle. By upholding our principles, we cultivate trust, respect and credibility in our personal and professional pursuits. The challenge is to find the delicate balance between ambition and maintaining our moral compass. By staying true to our values, we not only achieve success but also inspire and uplift others around us.

Upholding our core values is essential for several reasons. First and foremost, it allows us to maintain our integrity and authenticity. When we stay true to our values, we act with honesty, transparency and ethical behaviour. This builds trust and credibility in our personal and professional pursuits, which are vital for long-term success and meaningful relationships.

Maintaining our core values helps us make principled decisions. It ensures that our actions support our beliefs and convictions. By upholding our values, we navigate the challenges of the hustle with a moral compass, enabling us to make choices that align with our principles, even when faced with difficult circumstances or temptations.

In addition, our values serve as a source of strength and resilience. The hustle can be demanding and challenging, with pressures to compromise or cut corners. However, by remaining steadfast in our values, we gain the inner strength to persevere and overcome obstacles with integrity. Our values become the foundation upon which we build our resilience, allowing us to bounce back from setbacks and stay true to our purpose.

By embodying our core values, we become role models and inspire those around us. Our military background has positioned us as leaders, and by maintaining our values, we demonstrate the importance of character and ethics. Our actions speak louder than words, and when others see us navigating the challenges of the civilian world while staying true to our values, we become a source of inspiration and motivation for those who seek to achieve success with integrity.

Staying true to our values also fosters positive and authentic relationships. In the hustle, networking and building connections are essential, and by demonstrating integrity and selflessness, we attract like-minded individuals who share similar values. These connections become valuable support systems and sources of collaboration, enabling us to achieve our goals while surrounded by a community that shares our principles.

Our values also safeguard our mental and emotional well-being. When we act in alignment with our values, we experience a sense of inner harmony and fulfilment. We avoid the regret, guilt and internal conflict that may arise from compromising our principles. By prioritising our values, we create an environment of self-respect and self-care, which enhances our overall well-being and contributes to our long-term success.

Upholding our values in the hustle allows us to have a positive impact on the world around us. By embodying courage, integrity and selflessness, we become agents of positive change. Our actions and choices can inspire others to embrace their own values and act in accordance with them. By being a beacon of integrity, we contribute to creating a better and more ethical society.

Holding true to our values also builds a strong foundation for long-term success. In a world that often prioritises short-term gains and compromises, staying true to our values can set us apart and create a sustainable advantage. It positions us as individuals of integrity and reliability, which attracts opportunities and builds a positive reputation.

Maintaining our core values, whilst hustling, means that we ensure that our success is not just measured by external achievements, but also by the content of our character. It allows us to navigate the challenges of the civilian world with grace, authenticity and a sense of purpose. Our values guide us in making decisions, building relationships and pursuing meaningful goals. By upholding our principles, we not only achieve personal and professional success but also contribute to a better and more ethical society.

"The standard that you walk past,
is the standard you accept." – David Morrison

After a career of hearing every CO and RSM within earshot spout this quote off, it's still one of my favourites, and is a powerful sacred utterance. In this instance though, I'm not referring to the standard of your 'areas', I'm talking to the standards of your (micro and macro) environmental 'values'! Sadly, all too often I've seen civilian organisations go through 'box-ticking exercises' when it comes to values. It turns out that values like being honest, having integrity, respecting others are in high demand. Enter the service leaver! Being great at your job and a nice person … Win, win.

CHAPTER 5
Apply Processes Taught from a Military Career

"Efficiency is doing things right; effectiveness
is doing the right things." – Peter Drucker

Military service equips us with invaluable processes and methodologies that can be applied to the hustle. From strategic planning to execution, these military-tested approaches provide a competitive advantage in the civilian realm. By adapting and leveraging these processes to suit our new environment, we can optimise our efforts, minimise errors and achieve greater effectiveness. Embracing the tried-and-tested strategies from our military careers empowers us to navigate the challenges of the hustle with confidence and purpose.

One of the key processes that military service instils in us is strategic planning. In the military, planning is meticulous and comprehensive, considering various factors and contingencies. This disciplined approach to planning can be directly applied to the hustle. By setting clear goals, identifying potential obstacles and developing strategic action plans, we can ensure that our efforts are focused and purposeful. Strategic planning allows us to align our actions with our long-term objectives, enabling us to make informed decisions and adapt to changing circumstances.

Another valuable process from our military background is effective communication. In the military, communication is precise, concise and efficient, leaving no room for misinterpretation. Applying this skill to the hustle allows us to convey our ideas, intentions and expectations clearly and effectively. By communicating with clarity and confidence, we can build strong professional relationships, collaborate effectively with others and negotiate successfully. Effective communication is a powerful tool that helps us navigate through the complexities of the civilian world and achieve our objectives.

The military teaches us the importance of discipline and accountability. The hustle demands self-discipline and a strong sense of personal responsibility. By applying the principles of discipline learned in the military, we can stay focused, organised and committed to our goals. We understand the significance of consistently putting in the effort, even when faced with obstacles or setbacks. This discipline ensures that we remain dedicated and persevere through challenges, increasing our chances of success.

In addition to discipline, the military inculcates adaptability and flexibility. The ability to adjust plans and strategies as circumstances change is crucial. The military teaches us to think on our feet, make quick decisions and adjust our approach as needed. By embracing this flexibility, we can navigate the unpredictable nature of the civilian world, seize opportunities and overcome unexpected challenges. The adaptability instilled in us during our military service allows us to thrive in dynamic environments and find innovative solutions to problems.

The military also instils the value of teamwork and collaboration. The ability to work effectively with others is essential, where partnerships and networks play a significant role in achieving success. The military teaches us to leverage the strengths of our team members, communicate efficiently and foster a sense of camaraderie. By applying these principles, we can build strong professional relationships, collaborate with others and achieve shared goals. The power of teamwork allows us to accomplish more than we could on our own, creating a multiplier effect.

We've learnt to naturally be proactive and take initiative. Opportunities often go to those who actively seek them out and take decisive action. By applying the proactive mindset learned in the military, we can identify and seize opportunities, position ourselves for success and create our own path. Taking initiative demonstrates our drive, ambition and resourcefulness, setting us apart in the competitive landscape of the civilian world.

Additionally, the military highlights the importance of continuous learning and improvement. A growth mindset is crucial for staying ahead and adapting to evolving circumstances. It's within our nature to embrace a mentality of constant learning, seeking out opportunities for professional development and refining our skills. By applying this approach to the hustle, we can stay updated on industry trends, acquire new knowledge and improve our capabilities. Continuous learning empowers us to innovate, remain competitive and achieve long-term success.

Another valuable process from our military experience is the emphasis on thoroughness and attention to detail. In the military, precision and accuracy are paramount, as even the smallest details can have significant consequences. By applying this level of meticulousness to the hustle, we ensure that our work is of high quality, free from errors and meets the expectations of others. Attention to detail not only reflects our professionalism but also instils confidence in those who work with us.

As veterans, we know the importance of resilience and mental fortitude. The hustle can be challenging, with setbacks and failures along the way. However, the resilience instilled in us during our military service enables us to bounce back, learn from failures and keep moving forward. We understand that setbacks are part of the journey, and with determination and perseverance, we can overcome obstacles and achieve our goals.

The military emphasises the significance of self-care and well-being. It is crucial to maintain our physical and mental health to sustain long-term success. We know the importance of self-discipline, physical fitness and mental resilience. By prioritising self-care, we ensure that we have the energy, focus and well-being necessary to navigate the challenges of the hustle and maintain a healthy work-life balance.

The processes and methodologies ingrained in us through our military service provide us with a unique advantage. By applying strategic planning, effective communication, discipline, adaptability, teamwork, proactivity, continuous learning, attention to detail, resilience and self-care, we can optimise our efforts and achieve success in the civilian realm. The lessons from our military careers serve as a foundation for our journey, enabling us to navigate with confidence, purpose and resilience.

CHAPTER 6
Being Ruthlessly Efficient

"There is always a better way to do something. Find it."
– Thomas A. Edison

The hustle demands efficiency in every aspect of our lives. It requires us to eliminate distractions, focus on high-value tasks and maximise productivity. By honing our time-management skills, setting clear goals and prioritising effectively, we can streamline our efforts and achieve remarkable results. Being ruthlessly efficient empowers us to make the most of every opportunity and propel ourselves toward success.

One crucial aspect of being ruthlessly efficient is mastering time management. Time is a precious resource that must be utilised wisely. By setting clear objectives and breaking them down into actionable tasks, we can create a roadmap for success. Effective time management involves identifying priorities, scheduling tasks and allocating resources appropriately. It allows us to focus our energy on high-value activities and eliminate time-wasting activities that do not contribute to our goals.

Being ruthlessly efficient requires us to eliminate distractions and maintain a laser-like focus. The hustle is filled with countless distractions, such as social media, excessive multitasking and unproductive meetings. By consciously minimising these distractions and creating an environment conducive to deep work, we can dedicate our full attention and energy to the tasks at hand. This level of focus enhances our productivity and enables us to accomplish more in less time.

In addition, being ruthlessly efficient means taking advantage of technology and automation. The digital age provides us with numerous tools and resources that can streamline our processes and save valuable time. Whether it's project management software, task automation tools or communication platforms, leveraging technology allows us to work smarter, not harder. By embracing these tools and adapting them to our specific needs, we can eliminate manual and repetitive tasks, freeing up time for more strategic and meaningful work.

Continue to set clear goals and objectives. Without a clear direction, our efforts can become scattered and unfocused. By defining specific, measurable, attainable, relevant and time-bound (SMART) goals, we create a roadmap that guides our actions and decisions. Clear goals provide us with a sense of purpose and motivation, helping us prioritise our tasks and make informed choices. They serve as a compass, keeping us on track and ensuring that our efforts are aligned with our desired outcomes.

Another aspect of being ruthlessly efficient is learning to delegate and outsource tasks when necessary. We cannot do everything ourselves, nor should we try to. By identifying tasks that can be delegated or outsourced, we free up our time and energy to focus on higher-level responsibilities. Delegating tasks to capable individuals allows us to leverage their skills and expertise, while outsourcing tasks to external professionals can provide specialised support and efficiency. Effective delegation and outsourcing ensure that our efforts are directed toward activities that truly require our unique abilities.

Prioritise effectively. Not all tasks are created equal, and not all tasks contribute equally to our goals. By adopting a mindset of ruthless prioritisation, we can identify the most important and impactful tasks and allocate our time and resources accordingly. This involves assessing tasks based on their urgency, importance and potential impact, and making conscious choices about what deserves our immediate attention. By focusing on high-value tasks, we ensure that our efforts generate the maximum return on investment.

Continuously evaluate and optimise your processes. The hustle is dynamic, and what worked yesterday may not work today. By regularly reviewing your workflows, identifying bottlenecks and seeking opportunities for improvement, you can refine your processes and eliminate inefficiencies. This mindset of continuous improvement allows us to adapt to changing circumstances, seize emerging opportunities and stay ahead in a competitive landscape.

Some time ago, I actively decided that I wanted to set up a company and work for myself. After spending time learning about the process of setting up my own company and the mechanics of how I might get paid, I started the ball rolling. I surrounded myself with people that believed in me and were able to support the move.

As with any transition, there was always an element of risk. I put as many mitigations in place as possible to ensure that if things went sour, I would be covered. But I've always been a firm believer in 'no risk, no reward'.

CHAPTER 7
Milk and Honey

"The hustle leads us to the land of milk and honey, where dreams become reality." – Anonymous

The culmination of our journey through the hustle brings us to the land of milk and honey, where our dreams manifest into reality. By embracing the hustle's mindset, consistently striving for growth and leveraging our unique skills and experiences, we position ourselves for extraordinary success. This chapter explores the sweet rewards that await us when we unlock our potential and seize the opportunities that come our way. It is in this land of milk and honey that we find fulfilment, purpose and the realisation that the hustle was always within us, waiting to be unleashed.

In the land of milk and honey, we witness our dreams manifesting into reality. Through resolute dedication and unyielding effort, we begin to see the fruits of our labour. We achieve the goals we set out to accomplish, whether it be in our professional endeavours or personal aspirations. The land of milk and honey represents a place of special importance, where we experience the tangible results of our hard work and resilience.

In this realm, we discover a renewed sense of purpose. The hustle not only brings financial rewards but also ignites a passion within us. The land of milk and honey is a place where our work becomes purpose-driven, where we make a positive impact on others, and where our efforts contribute to a greater cause.

The sacred land of milk and honey is a testament to the growth and transformation we undergo throughout our hustle journey. As we push ourselves beyond our comfort zones, embrace challenges and constantly learn and improve, we evolve into versions of ourselves that we never thought possible. It is a place where we continuously strive for personal and professional growth, reaching new heights and surpassing our own expectations.

In the land of milk and honey, we become beacons of inspiration for others. Our success becomes a testament to the power of the hustle and serves as a source of motivation for those who aspire to achieve greatness. By sharing our stories, lessons and insights, we inspire and uplift others, empowering them to embark on their own hustle journeys and unlock their potential. The land of milk and honey becomes a community where like-minded individuals come together, supporting and uplifting one another on their paths to success.

Through our pursuit of success, we create opportunities for ourselves, forging our own paths and charting our destinies. We no longer rely on external circumstances or the decisions of others to determine our fate. Instead, we take control of our lives, making choices that align with our values and aspirations. The land of milk and honey is a place where we have the power to shape our own future and live life on our own terms.

Additionally, in this realm, we experience the joy of abundance. The hustle opens doors to new opportunities, connections and possibilities. We find ourselves surrounded by abundance in all its forms – financial prosperity, personal growth, meaningful relationships and a sense of purpose. The land of milk and honey is a place where we no longer feel limited by scarcity but rather thrive in a world of infinite possibilities.

The land of milk and honey is a reminder of the resilience and determination that carried us through the challenges of the hustle. It is a testament to our ability to overcome obstacles, persevere in the face of adversity and bounce back from setbacks. In this land, we recognise the strength and tenacity that reside within us, empowering us to push through difficult times and emerge stronger than before.

This special place serves as a constant reminder that success is not a destination but an ongoing journey. As we achieve one goal, we set our sights on new aspirations, continuing to push ourselves to new heights. The land of milk and honey is a place where we embrace a mindset of continuous growth and improvement, never settling for mediocrity but always striving for excellence.

Through embracing the hustle's mindset, consistently striving for growth, and leveraging our unique skills and experiences, we position ourselves for extraordinary success. The land of milk and honey is a testament to the boundless possibilities that await us when we dare to unlock our true potential and seize the opportunities that come our way.

CHAPTER 8
THE HUSTLE

"The dream is free, but the hustle is sold separately."
– Anonymous

As you embark on your post-military journey, it is important to remember that the hustle is not an elusive concept reserved for a select few. Instead, it is a mindset that is available to all individuals who dare to pursue their dreams and unleash their full potential. By embracing the hustle's unrelenting pursuit, you set yourself on a path of continuous growth and achievement.

Recognising your worth is a crucial aspect of the hustle. As a military service leaver, it is easy to underestimate your value in the civilian world. However, you possess a unique set of skills, discipline and resilience that few can match. By acknowledging your worth and refusing to settle for anything less than what you deserve, you empower yourself to seize opportunities that align with your true potential.

Shedding the constraints of rank is another key principle. While the military operates within a hierarchical structure, the civilian world knows no rank. It is up to you to let go of the limitations imposed by previous military roles and embrace a mindset that values merit, initiative and results. By focusing on your capabilities and achievements, you can redefine success on your own terms and forge your own path.

Staying true to your values is paramount as you navigate the hustle. The military instils core values such as courage, discipline, integrity and selflessness. By upholding these principles, you cultivate trust, respect and credibility in your personal and professional pursuits. The hustle challenges you to find a delicate balance between ambition and maintaining your moral compass, ensuring that your success is not achieved at the expense of your integrity.

Leveraging the processes and methodologies learned during your military career is a valuable asset in the hustle. From strategic planning to execution, these military-tested approaches provide a competitive advantage in the civilian realm. By adapting and applying these processes to suit your new environment, you can optimise your efforts, minimise errors and achieve greater effectiveness. Embracing the strategies and disciplines learned in the military empowers you to navigate the challenges of the hustle with confidence and purpose.

Cultivating ruthless efficiency is a fundamental aspect of the hustle. It demands that you eliminate distractions, focus on high-value tasks and maximise productivity. By honing your time-management skills, setting clear goals and prioritising effectively, you can streamline your efforts and achieve remarkable results. Being ruthlessly efficient allows you to make the most of every opportunity and propel yourself toward success.

As you embrace the hustle, let it become your ally in your pursuit of success. By adopting a hustler's mindset, recognising your worth, shedding the constraints of rank, staying true to your values, leveraging military processes, cultivating ruthless efficiency and seeking your own version of milk and honey, you unlock your true potential and fulfil your highest aspirations. The hustle is not a distant concept; it is within your reach. Let it guide you on your journey, and success will be yours to conquer.

ABOUT THE AUTHOR

Matt, a determined and driven individual, was born and raised in the historic town of Colchester, Essex. Having spent eleven years serving in the British Army (Royal Corps of Signals), Matt developed a deep sense of discipline, resilience and a passion for pushing beyond boundaries. Upon leaving the Army, he embarked on a remarkable journey, defying conventional paths and carving out his own unique success story.

With an entrepreneurial spirit, Matt ventured into uncharted territories, establishing a diverse portfolio of businesses that showcased his versatility and relentless commitment. Undeterred by the challenges that lay ahead, he fearlessly pursued his ambitions, self-funding each venture with sheer determination and drive.

Recognising the value of his military training and experiences, Matt harnessed the skills acquired during his service and applied them to the corporate world. He established a thriving consulting company, offering strategic guidance and expertise to organisations seeking transformation and growth. Drawing from his own leadership background, he seamlessly transitioned into an executive coaching practice, empowering individuals to unleash their full potential and excel in their professional journeys.

Embracing yet another domain, Matt ventured into the world of property development. Through meticulous planning, shrewd investments and a keen eye for opportunities, he navigated the complexities of the real estate market, turning dreams into tangible assets. Undeniably, his work ethic and entrepreneurial acumen proved instrumental in this venture's success.

Driven by a constant thirst for innovation and a fascination with technology, Matt embarked on a new frontier: founding his own tech start-up. With limited resources but an abundance of determination, he hustled tirelessly to bring his ideas to life. Guided by a belief in the transformative power of technology, Matt forged ahead, fuelling his start-up's growth through his dedication and resourcefulness.

Matt's journey is an inspiring testament to the power of persistence and resilience. His story exemplifies the possibilities that arise when one chooses to embrace the unknown, challenge convention and pursue dreams with determination.

In *The Hustle: Unleashing Your Potential Beyond Military Service*, Matt shares his wealth of knowledge, experiences and hard-earned wisdom. With candour and authenticity, he imparts valuable lessons on harnessing the unique strengths developed during military service and applying them to create extraordinary success in the civilian world. Matt's insights, born from the trenches of his own hustle, will inspire readers to embrace their full potential and boldly forge their own paths.

As you embark on this transformative journey through the pages of *The Hustle*, prepare to be inspired, motivated and empowered to unleash your true potential beyond the constraints of your own history.

Printed in Great Britain
by Amazon